Animal Offspring

Elephants and Their Calves

Revised Edition

by Margaret Hall

Consulting Editor: Gail Saunders-Smith, Ph.D.

Consultant: Carol Buckley, Executive Director
The Elephant Sanctuary
Hohenwald, Tennessee

CAPSTONE PRESS
a capstone imprint

Pebble Plus is published by Capstone Press
1710 Roe Crest Drive, North Mankato, Minnesota 56003
www.mycapstone.com

Library of Congress Cataloging-in-Publication Data is available on the Library of Congress website.
ISBN: 978-1-5157-4236-4 (paperback)
ISBN: 978-1-5157-4351-4 (ebook pdf)

Editorial Credits
Sarah L. Schuette, editor; Kia Adams, series designer; Jenny Schonborn, cover production designer;
Kelly Garvin, photo researcher; Eric Kudalis, product planning editor

Photo Credits
Minden Pictures: Konrad Wothe, 11; Shutterstock: Alta Oosthuizen, 19, Andre Klopper, left 21, Anke van Wyk, Cover, Four Oaks, 5, 17, J Reineke, right 21, Johan Swanepoel, 7, 15, JONATHAN PLEDGER, right 20, Kirill Trubitsyn, 13, Maggy Meyer, left 20, Steve Bower, 1

Note to Parents and Teachers

The Animal Offspring series supports national science standards related to life science. This book describes and illustrates elephants and their calves. The images support early readers in understanding the text. The repetition of words and phrases helps early readers learn new words. This book also introduces early readers to subject-specific vocabulary words, which are defined in the Glossary section. Early readers may need assistance to read some words and to use the Table of Contents, Glossary, Read More, Internet Sites, and Index/Word List sections of the book.

Word Count: 103
Early-Intervention Level: 12

Printed in the United States   6042

Table of Contents

Elephants

Elephants are large mammals with trunks and tusks. Young elephants are called calves.

Elephants and their calves

live in Africa and Asia.

A male elephant is a bull.

A female elephant is a cow.

Bulls and cows mate.

The Calf

Most cows give birth
to one calf at a time.
A group of cows protects
the calf.

Calves drink milk
from their mothers.
They start to eat plants
after a few months.

Calves play. Calves learn

how to use their trunks.

Growing Up

Male calves leave their mothers after five years. Bulls live alone.

Female calves stay
with their mothers. Cows live
together in family groups
called herds.

Watch Elephants Grow

birth

adult after about 20 years

Glossary

Africa—one of the seven continents of the world

Asia—the largest continent in the world

herd—a group of animals that lives or moves together

mammal—a warm-blooded animal that has a backbone and hair or fur; female mammals feed milk to their young; elephants are the largest land mammals on Earth.

mate—to join together to produce young

protect—to guard or keep safe from harm

trunk—a long nose; an elephant uses its trunk to bring food and water into its mouth.

tusk—a long, pointed tooth; all elephants have two tusks, except for female Asian elephants.

Read More

Buckley, Carol. *Travels with Tarra.* Gardiner, Maine: Tilbury House Publishers, 2002.

Crossingham, John, and Bobbie Kalman. *What Is an Elephant?* The Science of Living Things. New York: Crabtree, 2002.

Richardson, Adele. *Elephants: Trunks and Tusks.* The Wild World of Animals. Mankato, Minn.: Bridgestone Books, 2002.

Internet Sites

Do you want to find out more about elephants and their calves? Let FactHound, our fact-finding hound dog, do the research for you!

Here's how:

1) Visit *http://www.facthound.com*

2) Type in the **Book ID** number: **0736821074**

3) Click on **FETCH IT**.

FactHound will fetch Internet sites picked by our editors just for you!

Index/Word List